THE ULTIMATE

Sky

FACTS

for Kids, Teens, & Adults

Explore Amazing Birds, Soaring Planes, Breathtaking Clouds, Wild Weather, and Fascinating Facts—From Nature to Flying Machines and Aviation Wonders!

Book 9 of Eleven Worlds to Explore
Ethereal Ray

Copyright © 2025 Ethereal Ray
All rights reserved.

No part of this publication may be reproduced, stored in a retrieval system, or transmitted in any form or by any means, electronic, mechanical, photocopying, recording, or otherwise, without the prior written permission of the author, except for brief quotations in reviews or scholarly analysis.

Images from Freepik

Table of Contents

Chapter 1: The Sky Above Us!..1

Chapter 2: Birds of the Sky: Flyers and Grounded Wonders.....7

Chapter 3: Soaring Through the Clouds 18

Chapter 4: Amazing Airplanes 23

Chapter 5: Hot Air Balloons, Blimps, and Strange Flying Machines 32

Chapter 6: Extreme Weather Wonders 39

Chapter 7: Creatures That Fly (But Aren't Birds) 47

Chapter 8: Sky Careers - Jobs That Reach for the Clouds 53

Chapter 9: Myths, Legends & Mysteries of the Sky 58

Chapter 10: The Future of the Sky...68

Sky Explorer Lab..75

The Ultimate Sky Quiz 83

Glossary of Sky Terms...93

What's YOUR Sky Discovery?..96

Review Request..98

Hi there, sky explorer! I'm **Zephyr**, and this is my feathery, high-flying buddy **Nimbus**!

We've had a blast guiding you through the wonders above. From clouds and creatures to flying machines and mysteries of the sky, we hope this journey filled your mind with curiosity and your heart with wonder.

If you loved soaring through the skies with us, maybe you could ask a grown-up to leave a review on Amazon? Your kind words help us keep exploring and creating even more awesome sky adventures for curious readers like you!

Until next time—keep your eyes on the skies!

Scan the QR below!

> "The sky is the daily bread of the eyes."
>
> -Ralph Waldo Emerson

Get ready to take off on an unforgettable journey through the wonders of the sky!

The Ultimate Sky Facts for Kids, Teens, & Adults: Explore Amazing Birds, Soaring Planes, Breathtaking Clouds, Wild Weather, and Fascinating Facts—From Nature to Flying Machines and Aviation Wonders! is bursting with fascinating facts, breathtaking illustrations, and sky-high stories designed to captivate curious minds of all ages.

This isn't just a book—it's your passport to the skies:

- **Fuel your imagination:** Fly alongside birds, glide through glowing clouds, and zoom through history's wildest flying inventions—from hot air balloons to rockets!

- **Learn and soar:** Discover how the atmosphere works, how animals fly (even the strange ones that aren't birds!), and how humans conquered the skies with innovation and bravery.

- **Explore the unknown:** Dive into myths, legends, and unsolved mysteries of the sky—from glowing sky creatures to UFOs and ancient sky gods.

- **Inspire discovery:** Share the experience with your family! From fun facts to future careers in the sky, this book offers something amazing on every page.

Whether you're a stargazer, a storm watcher, or just someone who loves looking up—this book will spark wonder, knowledge, and imagination like never before.

So grab your wings (and your imagination), because your sky-high adventure is about to begin!

Chapter 1:
The Sky Above Us!

"Hey there, explorer! I'm **Zephyr**, your guide through the skies, and this is **Nimbus**— my feathery best friend with the fluffiest wings you'll ever see.

The sky above us is more than just blue... it's a swirling, soaring, ever-changing world, and today we're diving right into it!

Buckle your seatbelt—or your wings—because this journey is about to take flight!"

Ethereal Ray

☁ What Is the Sky?

Look up. That endless blue canvas above your head? That's the sky—and it's more magical than you think.

The sky isn't just "empty space." It's a vast, ever-changing world filled with movement, color, light, and life. It begins right above you and stretches all the way into space! The sky is made up of layers of gases called the **atmosphere**, and it's bursting with fascinating things to discover.

🌐 Why Is the Sky So Important?

The sky plays a huge role in keeping Earth livable and beautiful. Here's why it matters:

- **The Air We Breathe**: Oxygen, nitrogen, and other invisible gases fill the sky—we need them to survive!
- **Weather Maker**: Rain, snow, sunshine, wind, and wild storms are all brewed up in the sky.
- **Sunlight Filter**: The sky protects us from harmful rays and helps regulate Earth's temperature.

- **A Natural Show**: From cotton-candy clouds to fiery sunsets, the sky puts on a breathtaking display every day.

What's Up There?

There's more floating, flying, and zooming around than you might think!

- **Clouds**: Made of water droplets or ice, clouds come in many shapes—like wispy cirrus or towering thunderheads.
- **Birds**: From hummingbirds to eagles, many birds soar high and travel vast distances across the sky.
- **Planes & Aviation Wonders**: Humans fly too! From jets to hot air balloons, we've found countless ways to join the sky's traffic.
- **Weather Phenomena**: Lightning, hail, tornadoes, and rainbows—all sky-born wonders!
- **Stars & Space**: At night, the sky transforms into a window to space: planets, moons, stars, and even meteors streak across it.

The Sky's Secret Layers: Exploring the Atmosphere

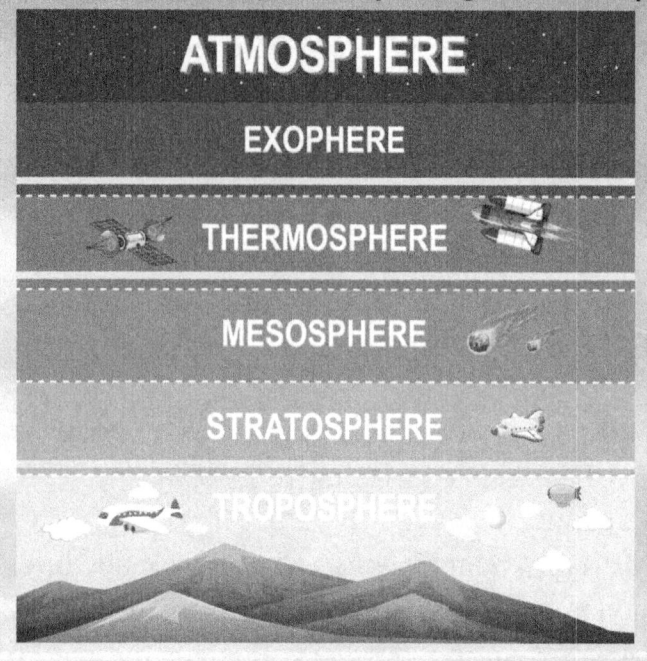

ATMOSPHERE
- EXOPHERE
- THERMOSPHERE
- MESOSPHERE
- STRATOSPHERE
- TROPOSPHERE

Just like the ocean has mysterious zones, the sky is made of invisible layers stacked on top of each other, each with its own vibe! These layers are what we call the **atmosphere**, and they stretch from the ground we walk on to the edge of space.

Let's take a high-flying trip through each one—from the breezy troposphere to the cosmic exosphere.

Troposphere – The Weather Layer (0-12 km / 0-7 miles)

- It's where we live, breathe, and watch clouds form.
- Almost all weather happens here—rain, snow, storms!
- Birds, balloons, and commercial airplanes hang out in this layer.

Stratosphere – The Jet Zone (12-50 km / 7-31 miles)

- Home to the ozone layer, which protects Earth from the Sun's harmful rays.
- Jet planes and some weather balloons fly here.
- Calm, clear, and cold—perfect for high-altitude flying.

Mesosphere – The Meteor Burner (50-85 km / 31-53 miles)

- Coldest layer in the atmosphere!
- Where meteors burn up—those "shooting stars" you see? Burnt up right here!
- Too high for planes, too low for satellites.

Thermosphere – The Space Border (85-600 km / 53-373 miles)

- Super thin air, but incredibly hot (over 1,000°C / 1,800°F)!
- This is where the Northern Lights dance in the sky.
- The International Space Station orbits here.

Exosphere – The Edge of Space (600+ km / 373+ miles)

- Practically space!
- Satellites drift here.
- You'd need a space suit—it's the last stop before outer space!

Fun Sky Facts

- Clouds can weigh **millions of pounds**—and still float!
- **Birds** can see ultraviolet light to help them navigate.

- **Some insects, like bees, can see patterns on flowers that are invisible to human eyes**—thanks to ultraviolet vision!
- **Planes take off against the wind** to lift better.
- The sky isn't actually blue—it just **looks** blue due to sunlight scattering!
- **Hot air rises**, so balloons float when the air inside is warmer than outside.
- The Sun looks yellow here, but it's actually **white** in space.
- Rainbows always appear **opposite the Sun**—turn your back to find one!

A Sky Full of Secrets

The sky holds mysteries and marvels: from jet stream winds that shape our weather to the shimmering dance of northern lights. It's where birds migrate, storms form, and people dream of flying farther.

It's not just science—it's adventure, imagination, and discovery all rolled into one.

Are You Ready to Fly?

From feathered friends and crazy clouds to roaring rockets and spinning storms, the sky has something for everyone.

So strap in, look up, and let your imagination take off—we're just getting started!

Chapter 2:
Birds of the Sky: Flyers and Grounded Wonders

"Wings up, friends! **Nimbus** and I are soaring alongside some of the most incredible creatures ever to take flight—**birds!**

From tiny flittering hummingbirds to soaring eagles that ride the wind, these feathery flyers rule the skies in their own brilliant ways.

Let's flap into the world of nests, beaks, migration routes, and sky-high superpowers!"

Why Birds Belong to the Sky

Birds are nature's most iconic sky travelers. They've evolved perfectly for flight with lightweight bones, feathers, and powerful wings. But did you know not all birds fly? Penguins swim, ostriches sprint—but even they carry the story of flight in their biology.

Birds fill every part of our skies—from cities to forests, mountains to coastlines. Their wings are as unique as their songs, shaped by millions of years of evolution to conquer different kinds of air.

The Science of Bird Flight

Birds don't just flap—they *fly* with skill! Here's how:

- **Lift & Wings:** Their wings are curved to push air downward, giving them lift (just like airplane wings!).

- **Feathers:** Lightweight, flexible, and waterproof—perfect for flight and staying warm.
- **Hollow Bones:** Strong yet light, so they can stay airborne longer without being weighed down.
- **Air Sacs:** Birds have special breathing systems with air sacs that let them take in oxygen even while exhaling—great for high altitudes!

Bird Records That Will Blow Your Mind

- **Fastest Bird in a Dive:** The peregrine falcon can reach speeds over **240 mph (386 km/h)**—faster than a race car!

- **Highest Flyer:** The Rüppell's griffon vulture has been recorded at **37,000 feet**—that's as high as a jet!

- **Longest Migration:** The Arctic tern travels from the Arctic to Antarctica and back—**over 44,000 miles** a year!

- **Biggest Wingspan:** The wandering albatross has wings that stretch up to **12 feet**—as wide as a car!

Birds Around the World

- **Rainforests:** Bright parrots and toucans call these skies home, using vivid colors to attract mates.

The Ultimate Sky Facts for Kids, Teens, & Adults

- **Mountains:** Eagles and condors glide on strong updrafts, spotting prey from far below.

- **Oceans:** Seabirds like gulls and puffins dive into the waves for fish and can spend days aloft.

- **Cities:** Pigeons, crows, and swifts have adapted to life around skyscrapers and streets.

Flight Patterns: From Flapping to Gliding

Birds have different flying styles:

- **Flapping:** Quick, rhythmic beats—like sparrows or finches.
- **Gliding:** Soaring with wings spread—like hawks or vultures.
- **Hovering:** Staying in one place midair—like hummingbirds!
- **Soaring:** Catching rising air currents (called thermals) and floating effortlessly.

Incredible Bird Adaptations

- Pigeons navigate using Earth's magnetic field and the Sun!

- Owls fly silently thanks to special feathers that reduce noise.

- Hummingbirds can fly backward—and their wings beat up to 80 times per second.

- Some parrots mimic human speech to communicate and bond.

- Snowy owls are perfectly camouflaged in icy tundras—stealthy sky hunters.

🦜 Flightless Birds: Earthbound, but Still Amazing

Not all birds take to the skies—but that doesn't make them any less incredible. Some have evolved to run fast, swim like pros, or survive in harsh environments without needing wings to fly.

Here are a few sky-connected creatures who prefer to stay grounded:

- 🐧 **Penguins**

They can't fly—but they "fly" through the water! Their wings have turned into flippers, helping them glide underwater with grace and speed.

Ethereal Ray

- 🐦 **Ostriches**

  The largest birds in the world. They can't fly, but they can run up to **45 miles per hour**, using their powerful legs to escape predators in the African savannah.

- 🐦 **Emus & Cassowaries**

  Native to Australia and nearby islands, these large, flightless birds are fast, strong, and in the cassowary's case—**seriously dinosaur-like.** (Cassowaries even have a helmet-like crest!)

- **Kiwis**

These shy, nocturnal birds from New Zealand have tiny wings and a long, sensitive beak. They mostly roam the forest floor, using smell to find insects—pretty rare for a bird!

Wings of Wonder

Birds have been gliding, flapping, and soaring across the sky long before humans ever dreamed of flying. From speedy falcons to flightless penguins, these feathered creatures show us that the sky is full of possibilities—even if you don't have wings that work! So next time you look up, see if you can spot a bird mid-flight... or maybe one waddling nearby with sky-high dreams of its own.

Chapter 3:
Soaring Through the Clouds

"Hold on tight—things are about to get fluffy!"

Nimbus just dove through a cotton-candy-looking cloud, and now we're surrounded by mist and magic.

Ever wondered what clouds are made of? Or how some can weigh more than elephants but still float?

Let's take a high-flying glide into the world of clouds, fog, mist, and the secrets they hold above our heads.

What *Are* Clouds, Anyway?

Clouds are made of teeny-tiny water droplets or ice crystals that float in the air. These droplets form when warm air rises, cools down, and the water vapor inside it condenses (that's a fancy word for turning into liquid). Boom! A cloud is born.

Even though they look light and fluffy, clouds can weigh *millions* of pounds. They float because the air around them is still lighter than they are—so up they go, riding on air currents!

The Different Types of Clouds (And What They Mean)

Clouds come in many shapes, heights, and personalities! Scientists sort them into three main groups based on how high they are in the sky—and each group has its own special cloud types.

Low-Level Clouds (Up to 6,500 feet)

- **Cumulus:** Big, puffy, and cottony. They usually mean fair weather—but when they grow tall, they can bring storms!
- **Stratus:** Flat, gray, and blanket-like. They often bring drizzles or gloomy skies.
- **Nimbostratus:** Thick and dark—these are the heavy rain or snow clouds.

Mid-Level Clouds (6,500-20,000 feet)

- **Altocumulus:** Small white or gray puffs in patches or rows. They can mean thunderstorms are on the way.
- **Altostratus:** Thin gray layers that cover the whole sky like frosted glass. They usually bring light rain or snow.

High-Level Clouds (Above 20,000 feet)

- **Cirrus:** Wispy and thin, like feathers or brush strokes. Made of ice crystals and often seen before changes in weather.
- **Cirrostratus:** Shiny and veil-like, they can create halos around the Sun or Moon!
- **Cirrocumulus:** Small white patches or ripples. These don't last long but look beautiful at sunrise or sunset.

Special Cloud Types

- **Cumulonimbus:** Towering and scary! These storm clouds can stretch from low to high altitudes and bring lightning, thunder, hail, and tornadoes.
- **Mammatus:** Bulging clouds that hang like pouches underneath other clouds—usually after a strong storm.

- **Lenticular:** UFO-shaped clouds that form near mountains. They're so strange, people often mistake them for alien ships!

Why Are Clouds So Many Colors?

Clouds can be white, gray, pink, orange—even greenish or purple! It all depends on the light:

- **White clouds** scatter all light evenly—so they look bright.
- **Dark clouds** are thicker and block more sunlight.
- **Sunsets and sunrises** paint clouds in red, orange, and pink because of how sunlight bends across the atmosphere.
- **Stormy clouds** sometimes look green or purple—that's a sign of powerful weather brewing!

Cloudy Curiosities and Fun Facts

- The average cumulus cloud weighs about *1.1 million pounds*!
- Pilots fly *above* storm clouds to avoid turbulence.
- The word *"cloud"* comes from an old English word that meant "rock" or "hill."
- There's a cloud on *Venus* made of sulfuric acid—definitely not fluffy or friendly!
- Clouds help regulate Earth's temperature by reflecting sunlight and trapping heat.

Ethereal Ray

🌥 Clouds & Weather: Nature's Clues

Nimbus says clouds are like the sky's mood ring—and he's right! You can actually predict the weather just by watching how clouds change:

- Puffy cumulus turning into tall thunderheads? A storm might be coming!
- A thin layer of cirrostratus? Rain might arrive within 24 hours.
- A sudden thickening of stratus clouds? Get your umbrella ready!

Farmers, sailors, and pilots have relied on clouds for centuries to read the sky.

🌥 Mini Activity: Name That Cloud!

Next time you're outside, look up and try to spot the different types. Can you tell the difference between cirrus and cumulus? Draw your favorite ones or take photos to compare.

Zephyr's Final Words:

Clouds may seem like soft fluff, but they carry clues about our planet, our weather, and even our future. Keeping your head in the clouds—in the best way—can help you notice the secret signs floating above us every day.

Chapter 4:
Amazing Airplanes

"Engines roaring, wings ready—prepare for takeoff!"
Nimbus and I are pulling up alongside some of the coolest flying machines humans have ever built.

From propellers to jet engines, let's discover how humans figured out the magic of flight—and the amazing science behind how metal birds soar across the sky.

Ethereal Ray

✈ What Is an Airplane?

An airplane is a machine that flies through the air using wings and engines. It's heavier than air (unlike a balloon), so it needs special forces to keep it up—like *lift*, *thrust*, *drag*, and *weight*. We'll break those down in a minute.

Airplanes come in all shapes and sizes:

- Small planes with just one seat
- Supersonic jets that travel faster than sound
- Giant cargo planes that carry tanks, cars, and even *other planes*!

☀ How Do Airplanes Fly?

Let's break it down with the **Four Forces of Flight**:

1. **Lift** - The force that pushes the plane *up*, created by air moving over and under the wings.
2. **Thrust** - The force that moves the plane *forward*, created by engines or propellers.

3. **Drag** – The air resistance that tries to slow the plane down.
4. **Weight** – The force of gravity pulling the plane down.

When lift beats weight, and thrust beats drag—boom! You're flying.

Fun Fact: The shape of an airplane wing is called an **airfoil**—curved on top and flatter underneath. This shape helps lift the plane by speeding up the air on top.

The Wright Brothers: First to Fly!

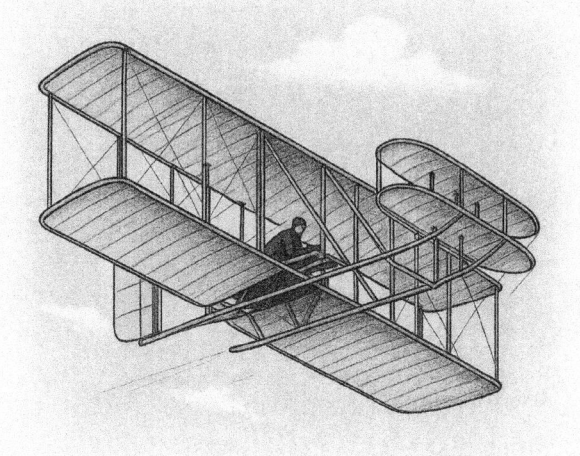

The Wright Flyer

In 1903, two bicycle makers named **Orville and Wilbur Wright** launched the world's first powered airplane in North Carolina. It was small, made of wood and cloth, and only flew for **12 seconds**—but it changed everything.

Ethereal Ray

Their plane was called the **Wright Flyer**, and even though it looked like a flying kite, it became the ancestor of every plane in the sky today.

✈ *Nimbus Fun Fact:* The Wright Flyer had no cockpit—it was flown lying down!

✈ **Different Types of Planes**

Let's explore the sky's variety pack:

✈ *Propeller Planes*

- Use spinning blades to create thrust.
- Great for short distances and stunts.
- Common in training, farming, and skywriting.

✈ Jet Planes

- Use jet engines to fly faster and higher.
- Commercial airliners like the Boeing 737 or Airbus A380 fall into this group.
- Some military jets can go *supersonic*—faster than sound!

✈ Cargo Planes

- Massive planes that carry goods instead of people.
- The Antonov An-225 was the heaviest aircraft ever built (it even carried a spaceship once!).

Ethereal Ray

✒ *Military Planes*

Air Force

- Built for speed, stealth, and power.
- Fighters like the F-22 Raptor or bombers like the B-2 Spirit are top-tier tech wonders.

✈ *Stunt Planes*

- Used in airshows for flips, loops, and barrel rolls.

- Small, agile, and incredibly tough.

🌐 Planes That Changed the World

- **Concorde** – A supersonic passenger jet that could fly from London to New York in under 3.5 hours!
- **Spirit of St. Louis** – Charles Lindbergh flew it solo across the Atlantic in 1927.
- **Voyager** – The first plane to fly around the world without stopping or refueling.
- **Solar Impulse 2** – A solar-powered plane that circled the globe using only sunlight!

🛠 Inside an Airplane

Modern airplanes are like flying cities:

- Cockpit: Where the pilots control everything.
- Engines: Jet or propeller, they power the plane.
- Wings: Lift generators.

- Tail: Helps with stability and direction.
- Cabin: Seats, food trays, windows, and sometimes movies!

✈ *Nimbus Note:* The tiny hole in airplane windows? That's on purpose—it keeps the pressure balanced and prevents fogging!

What's It Like to Fly?

At 35,000 feet, airplanes cruise high above the clouds where the air is thin and cold. The views? *Unbelievable.* You might see entire mountain ranges, sunsets that stretch forever, or lightning storms from above!

Sometimes you'll feel turbulence—that shaky feeling. It's just the plane moving through bumpy air. Pilots are trained to handle it, and planes are built to take it.

Mind-Blowing Plane Facts

- The fastest plane ever? The **SR-71 Blackbird**—over **2,100 mph!**
- The world's busiest airport is **Hartsfield-Jackson Atlanta International.**
- The **Boeing 747** has over **6 million parts.**
- **Pilots speak a global language** in the skies—aviation English.
- **Air traffic control** guides thousands of planes in the sky at once—it's like a giant 3D puzzle.

🎮 Zephyr's Flight Challenge:

Design your own airplane! What kind of wings will it have? Propeller or jet engine? Where will it fly? Bonus points if you give it a cool name (Nimbus named one "Sky Gobbler." We're... still working on that).

_____

✈ Zephyr's Final Words:

"Airplanes turned dreams of flying into reality—and opened the sky to the whole world. Whether you're soaring on vacation or imagining new aircraft of the future, remember: every great flight starts with a wild idea... and a spark of curiosity."

Chapter 5:
Hot Air Balloons, Blimps, and Strange Flying Machines

"Greetings again, sky explorers! I hope you're not afraid of heights, because in this chapter, we're floating above the world in some of the *strangest*, *roundest*, and *most delightful* sky machines ever invented.

From drifting balloons to blimps that look like sky whales—and even wild contraptions that *almost* worked—we're traveling through history, science, and a little bit of silliness.

Let's rise!"

The First Flyers: Hot Air Balloons

Before engines, wings, or jets, there were **balloons**.

In **1783**, two brothers named **Joseph and Étienne Montgolfier** launched the **first hot air balloon** in France. It soared over a crowd with *a sheep, a duck, and a rooster* as passengers! Why? Because they wanted to test flight *before risking a human*.

A few months later, a brave man named **Jean-François Pilâtre de Rozier** took the first *human* ride. He floated above Paris for 25 minutes in a woven basket.

Nimbus Fact: People thought flying in a balloon would change your brain because the sky was so mysterious. Luckily, no one turned into a sky goose.

How Hot Air Balloons Work

- A giant fabric envelope traps **hot air**.
- A burner heats the air, making it **lighter** than the cool air outside.

Ethereal Ray

- Since hot air rises, the balloon floats up!
- Pilots adjust the flame to go higher or lower, and the wind does the rest.

No steering wheel! Balloons go wherever the wind takes them. That's part of the adventure!

Famous Balloon Adventures

- **Around the World!** In 1999, **Bertrand Piccard and Brian Jones** flew nonstop around the globe in a balloon named *Breitling Orbiter 3*.
- **Extreme Heights!** In 2012, **Felix Baumgartner** rose 24 miles up in a helium balloon—then *jumped out*. He broke the sound barrier falling back to Earth!

What's a Blimp?

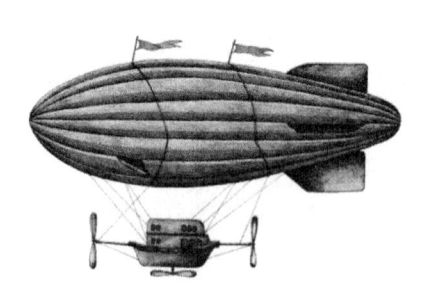

A **blimp** is a giant floating airship filled with a light gas—usually **helium**. Unlike hot air balloons, blimps can *steer*, thanks to engines and fins.

They look like flying whales with fins, and they move slowly and silently. Today, they're used for:

- TV coverage of sports games
- Advertising (like the famous Goodyear Blimp)
- Tourism and sky tours

☀ The Zeppelin Disaster

Early airships used **hydrogen**—which is lighter than air but also *very flammable*. In 1937, the **Hindenburg**, a massive German Zeppelin, caught fire while landing. The accident was tragic and marked the end of hydrogen airships.

Today, we use **helium**, which is much safer (and makes your voice squeaky).

😊 Strange Flying Machines from History

The sky has inspired **some weird ideas**. Not all of them worked—but they're fun to imagine.

🦋 Ornithopters

- Flying machines with **flapping wings**, like birds or insects.
- Leonardo da Vinci dreamed them up in the 1400s!
- Some inventors still try to make them work.

Ethereal Ray

🚴 Flying Bicycles

- Yup. Bicycles with wings or rotors.
- Many early designs failed... but modern *pedal-powered aircraft* have actually flown!

🪁 Human Kites

- Giant kites designed to lift people into the air.
- Used in ancient China and even in World War I for observation.

UFO Lookalikes

- Some inventors made flying saucers, hovering disks, or spinning tops.
- Most never left the ground, but they inspired movies and mystery stories.

💭 *Zephyr chuckles*: "Sometimes what *doesn't* fly is just as fun as what does!"

Lighter-Than-Air vs. Heavier-Than-Air

Type	Floats or Flies?	How It Works
Hot Air Balloon	Floats	Hot air is lighter than cool air
Blimp or Zeppelin	Floats	Gas (helium/hydrogen) lifts it
Airplane	Flies	Wings + thrust = lift

Type	Floats or Flies?	How It Works
Helicopter	Flies	Rotors push air down to go up
Strange Invention Thingy	??	Usually... crash!

Modern Floating Fun

- **Balloon Festivals** - Giant colorful balloons fill the sky in places like New Mexico's **Balloon Fiesta**.
- **Tourist Blimps** - Slow and scenic, some let you float over cities or coastlines.
- **Science Balloons** - NASA uses balloons to send instruments high above Earth for space research!

Imagine Your Own Flying Machine!

If you could design a floating sky vehicle:

- What would it be shaped like?
- What would lift it—helium, hot air, dreams?
- Would it have snacks onboard? (Nimbus says yes.)

Draw it. Name it. Dream it.

Zephyr's Final Words:

"The sky belongs not just to machines that roar, but to those that *float, drift,* and *delight.* Balloons and blimps remind us

Ethereal Ray

that flying isn't always about speed—it can be about wonder. Keep dreaming, inventing, and imagining the next strange thing to rise."

Chapter 6:
Extreme Weather Wonders

"You've soared through clouds and flown with birds—now brace yourselves!

The sky isn't always calm and dreamy. Sometimes, it puts on a wild, powerful show. From roaring thunder to swirling tornadoes, the atmosphere is constantly stirring up excitement (and a few goosebumps).

Come along as we zip through the most extreme weather wonders on Earth!"

What *Is* Weather, Anyway?

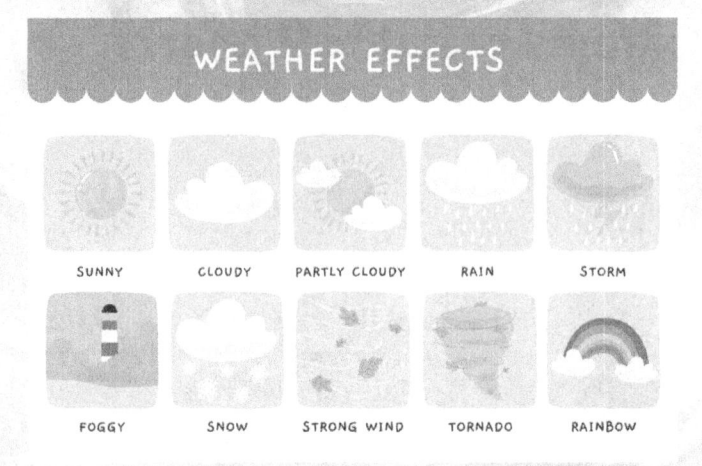

WEATHER EFFECTS

- SUNNY
- CLOUDY
- PARTLY CLOUDY
- RAIN
- STORM
- FOGGY
- SNOW
- STRONG WIND
- TORNADO
- RAINBOW

Weather is the day-to-day state of the atmosphere in a particular place. It includes temperature, humidity, wind, clouds, precipitation (rain, snow, hail), and atmospheric pressure.

- **Climate** is the average weather over a long period.
- **Weather** is what you get *right now*—sunny one moment, stormy the next!

Types of Weather—From Mild to Wild!

Let's take a tour through some of Earth's most powerful and fascinating weather phenomena:

Rain and Showers

Rain keeps our planet alive! It nourishes plants, fills rivers, and cleans the air.

- Light rain = drizzle
- Sudden rain bursts = showers
- Long, soaking rain = steady rainfall

Nimbus Fact: Raindrops aren't shaped like teardrops—they're more like hamburger buns as they fall!

Snow and Ice

Snowflakes form when water vapor freezes into crystals. Every snowflake is *unique*—no two are exactly alike!

- Blizzards: fierce snowstorms with powerful winds
- Sleet: frozen raindrops
- Hail: balls of ice that fall during strong thunderstorms

Nimbus Fact: The largest snowflake ever recorded was 15 inches wide—like a flying pizza!

Thunderstorms

Thunderstorms are dramatic and electric! They form when warm, moist air rises quickly.

- Lightning heats the air so fast it creates a shockwave—*boom!* That's thunder.
- A single lightning bolt can reach **30,000°C**—hotter than the surface of the sun!

Nimbus Fact: You can count the seconds between lightning and thunder to estimate how far away a storm is!

Tornadoes

Tornadoes are spinning columns of air that reach from a thunderstorm to the ground.

- Wind speeds can exceed **300 mph!**
- Tornado Alley in the U.S. sees the most twisters per year

Nimbus Fact: Tornadoes are ranked by the EF Scale (Enhanced Fujita)—EF0 (weakest) to EF5 (strongest)!

Hurricanes & Typhoons

These mighty storms form over warm ocean water. They're called:

- **Hurricanes** in the Atlantic,
- **Typhoons** in the Pacific,
- **Cyclones** in the Indian Ocean.

They can be hundreds of miles wide, bringing heavy rain, storm surges, and fierce winds!

Nimbus Fact: The eye of a hurricane is calm and clear, even while chaos swirls around it.

Fog and Mist

Fog is like a cloud that touches the ground. It forms when the air is cool and full of moisture.

- Mist is like baby fog—lighter and less dense.

Nimbus Fact: In some places like San Francisco, fog has a name—**Karl!**

Wind Power!

Wind happens when air moves from high-pressure to low-pressure areas. The bigger the difference, the stronger the wind!

- Gentle breeze: 1-15 mph
- Gale: 30-55 mph
- Hurricane-force wind: Over 75 mph!

Nimbus Fact: The fastest wind speed ever recorded on Earth (outside a tornado) was **253 mph** during Cyclone Olivia in 1996!

Bonus Wonder: Rainbows!

Rainbows form when sunlight passes through raindrops and gets split into colors. The result? Pure sky magic.

- A full rainbow is a circle—but we usually see just the top half.
- Double rainbows? That's light bouncing *twice* inside the raindrops!

Zephyr's Final Words:

"Whether it's a sizzling lightning bolt, a swirling tornado, or a quiet misty morning, weather is the sky's way of putting on a show! Next time you step outside, look up—you might catch something amazing happening right above your head."

Chapter 7: Creatures That Fly (But Aren't Birds)

"Think only birds rule the sky? Think again! The sky is full of life—fluttering, gliding, zooming creatures that fly in ways you might never expect.

From bats to butterflies, flying fish to dragonflies, we're about to meet some of the sky's most fascinating fliers that *aren't* birds. Let's lift off!"

Ethereal Ray

🦇 Bats: The Only Flying Mammals

Bats are the **only mammals** that can truly fly.

- Their wings are made of **skin stretched over finger bones**—like tiny umbrellas!
- They fly at night using **echolocation** (they bounce sound off objects to "see" in the dark)
- Some species eat insects, while others sip sweet fruit juice or nectar

Fun Fact: The **bumblebee bat** is the world's smallest mammal—it's *smaller than your thumb*!

🐞 Insects: Masters of Miniature Flight

Insects are **sky acrobats** with wings that buzz, zip, and flutter.

Here are some sky stars:

- **Butterflies** – Float gently and pollinate flowers
- **Dragonflies** – Can hover, dart, and fly backward!
- **Bees** – Tiny but powerful pollinators
- **Beetles** – Many have hard outer wings and fly using hidden ones underneath
- **Moths** – Night-flying cousins of butterflies

🍃 **Cool Note:** Some insects have **two wings** (like bees), while others have **four** (like dragonflies).

Nimbus says: "Dragonflies were once the size of eagles millions of years ago!" (Well... sort of. Fossils show they had **2-foot wingspans!**)

🪰 **How Do Insects Fly?**

Insects fly by flapping their wings incredibly fast—some hundreds of times **per second**!

- **Fruit flies** beat their wings ~200 times per second
- **Mosquitoes** buzz around 300-600 beats per second
- **Bee wings** are powered by *indirect muscles* inside their body—so the wings flap even when their muscles don't directly pull them

💧 That's why they sound like little motors!

Ethereal Ray

🌱 Flying Reptiles? Not Just Dinosaurs!

Some reptiles don't fly, but they **glide** through the air.

- **Flying dragons** (Draco lizards) have ribs that spread out like wings—they jump from trees and glide through the air
- **Flying snakes** flatten their bodies and wiggle in the air to glide from tree to tree (yes, really!)
- In the time of dinosaurs, **pterosaurs** were the kings of the sky—with wingspans from a bird-sized **pigeon** to the bus-sized **Quetzalcoatlus**!

🦴 **Fossil Fact:** Pterosaurs weren't dinosaurs or birds—they were their own flying group!

🐿️ Gliders of the Sky

Some mammals can't fly but they **glide** amazingly well:

- **Flying squirrels** have flaps of skin between their arms and legs. They leap from trees and glide for up to **300 feet (90 meters)**!
- **Colugos** (a.k.a. flying lemurs—not real lemurs!) are expert gliders from Southeast Asia

🧠 *Zephyr says:* "It's like nature invented its own flying suits!"

🐟 Flying Fish and Sky-Hopping Squid?!

Yes, some **ocean creatures** can *glide* through the air!

- **Flying fish** leap from the sea and glide on extended fins to escape predators (they can soar over **600 feet!** That's longer than a football field!)

Ethereal Ray

- **Flying squid** use jets of water to **launch** themselves above the waves and coast through the air—sometimes dozens leap together in glowing blue swarms

Nimbus adds: "It's like a flying parade from the sea!"

🐛 Bonus Sky Oddballs!

- **Gliding frogs** - Some tree frogs have webbed toes that work like parachutes
- **Jumping spiders** - Some can leap into the air and even "parachute" on silk threads!
- **Ballooning spiders** - Baby spiders ride the wind on silk strands, floating through the air like tiny sky travelers

Cool Term: This spider-flying trick is called **ballooning**—they can go as high as airplanes and travel miles!

💡 Zephyr's Final Words:

"Flying isn't just for birds. The sky belongs to anyone brave (or clever) enough to take to the air. From bats that dance through the night to dragonflies zipping through the day, the sky is buzzing with life. Remember—amazing things happen when you dare to take flight... no feathers required."

Chapter 8:
Sky Careers
- Jobs That Reach for the Clouds

"Wings ready, explorer? It's Zephyr and Nimbus again, gliding in with something a little different today!

Ever wondered who gets to study the sky, fly through it, or even protect it? From pilots to meteorologists, there are real people out there with sky-powered jobs—and one of them might be your future!"

Ethereal Ray

What Are Sky Careers?

Sky careers are jobs that take place *in the sky, about the sky*, or *because of the sky*! These exciting roles can involve flying, studying weather and space, building aircraft, or even keeping people safe up above.

✈ Pilot

What They Do: Fly airplanes—from small private jets to giant commercial planes.
Skills Needed: Quick thinking, focus, excellent training.
Fun Fact: Pilots talk to air traffic control using a special radio language!

Meteorologist

What They Do: Study and predict the weather. They use satellites, radar, and computer models to track storms, winds, and more.
Skills Needed: Science, math, observation.

Fun Fact: The word "meteorologist" comes from the Greek word *meteoros*, meaning "high in the sky."

🛰 Aerospace Engineer

What They Do: Design aircraft, rockets, and satellites. These are the people who figure out how to make things fly safely and efficiently.
Skills Needed: Engineering, creativity, problem-solving.
Fun Fact: Some engineers even work on space tourism rockets!

🎈 Balloonist & Paraglider

What They Do: These adventurous sky travelers fly using hot air balloons or paragliders!
Skills Needed: Navigation, training, safety awareness.
Fun Fact: The first humans to fly were balloonists in the 1700s—before airplanes!

🚁 Air Traffic Controller

What They Do: Help pilots take off, land, and stay safe in the skies by guiding them from control towers.
Skills Needed: Communication, attention to detail, calm under pressure.
Fun Fact: They manage thousands of planes in the air at once—like a traffic cop for the sky!

Ethereal Ray

🦅 Ornithologist

What They Do: Study birds, their flight, migration, and behavior.
Skills Needed: Biology, fieldwork, patience.
Fun Fact: Some ornithologists track birds with tiny GPS devices to follow their journeys!

🔧 Aircraft Mechanic

What They Do: Make sure planes and helicopters are safe and ready to fly.
Skills Needed: Mechanical skills, precision, and technical training.
Fun Fact: Mechanics often inspect hundreds of parts before every flight!

🚀 Astronaut

What They Do: Travel to space and live beyond Earth's sky!
Skills Needed: Science, physical fitness, bravery.
Fun Fact: Astronauts train in giant swimming pools to practice working in zero gravity!

🌎 Environmental Scientist (Sky Edition)

What They Do: Study air pollution, climate change, and how the atmosphere affects Earth.
Skills Needed: Research, environmental science, tech tools.
Fun Fact: Some use sky drones to monitor pollution or weather from above!

🌟 Bonus: Sky Communicators

These are educators, authors (like you!), illustrators, and museum guides who teach others about the sky—turning curiosity into inspiration.

How Can You Start?

- Stay curious—ask questions and explore.
- Read about weather, planes, and stars.
- Try science projects, flight simulators, or birdwatching.
- Visit museums, airports, or planetariums.
- Dream big—your sky career starts with imagination!

Zephyr's Wrap-Up:
"The sky isn't just a place to dream—it's a place to work, learn, and explore. Whether you want to fly through the clouds, build the next space shuttle, or simply teach others about the wonders above—there's a sky path waiting just for you. So... which one calls to you?"

Chapter 9:
Myths, Legends & Mysteries of the Sky

"Things are getting mysterious up here..."

Nimbus swears he just saw a flying dragon—but maybe it was just a cloud shaped like one? Around the world, people have told sky stories for centuries.

From thunder gods to UFO sightings, let's uncover the myths, legends, and curious mysteries that keep our heads turned skyward.

🏛 Legendary Skies from Around the World

For centuries, people all over the world have looked up and told stories about what they saw. Here are some of the most magical:

- **The Sun Chariot (Greece):** Ancient Greeks believed the Sun was pulled across the sky by a golden chariot driven by Helios.
- **Thunderbirds (Native American):** Giant birds that flapped their wings to create thunder and lightning. They were considered powerful spirit protectors.
- **The Sky Woman (Iroquois legend):** A woman fell from the sky world and created the Earth with the help of animals.
- **Ra, the Sun God (Egypt):** Ra sailed across the sky in a solar boat, bringing light during the day and traveling through the underworld at night.
- **The Rainbow Serpent (Aboriginal Australia):** A powerful being who created rivers and mountains and travels through the sky after storms.

- **Chinese Sky Dragons:** Unlike Western dragons, these flying serpents were lucky, wise, and often associated with rain and clouds.

Constellations & Stories in the Stars

Long ago, people saw pictures in the stars—called **constellations**—and turned them into epic tales:

- **Orion the Hunter** - A mighty figure chased across the sky by the Scorpion.
- **Pegasus** - A flying horse born from a magical sea creature.
- **Ursa Major & Minor** - Bears placed in the sky by gods, with the North Star at their tail.
- **The Milky Way** - Many cultures saw this band of stars as a road: a spirit path, a river, or a trail of stardust.

Even today, stargazing connects us with these old stories!

Mysterious Sky Phenomena

Not everything in the sky is easily explained. Some things still leave us scratching our heads...

- **Ball lightning** – Glowing orbs of electricity that float in the air during storms? Scientists still aren't sure how they work!
- **Sprites & Elves** – No, not the fairytale kind! These are colorful flashes high above thunderstorms that look like sky jellyfish.
- **Sundogs** – Bright spots on either side of the Sun, often seen in cold weather. They look like mini suns!
- **UFOs (Unidentified Flying Objects)** – Strange shapes and lights in the sky that people can't explain... yet.

Most have logical explanations, but the mystery still excites the imagination!

Sky Symbols & Beliefs

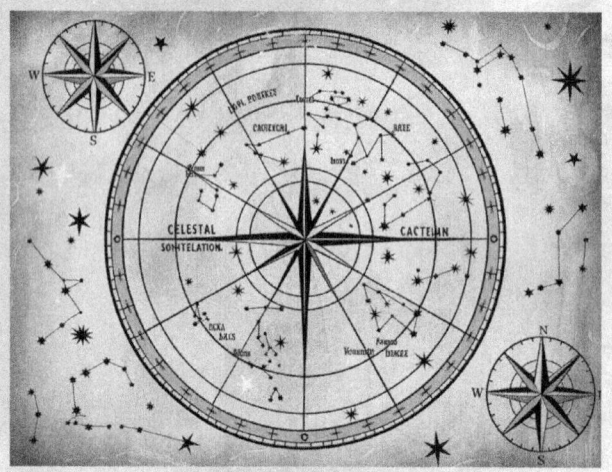

- **Rainbows** - A promise, a path to another world, or a sign of peace, depending on the culture.
- **Eclipses** - Once feared as omens or sky monsters swallowing the Sun or Moon!
- **The Northern Lights (Aurora Borealis)** - Some believed they were dancing spirits or bridges to the heavens.
- **Meteor Showers** - Called "falling stars," they've been wished upon for centuries.

Creatures of Myth & Mystery

The sky isn't just home to stars and storms—it's also where some of the most legendary creatures ever imagined took flight! Some are based on real animals. Others? Pure imagination. But all of them live in the stories we still tell today.

The Ultimate Sky Facts for Kids, Teens, & Adults

🦤 The Dodo: A Flightless Legend

The dodo never soared through the clouds, but its story sure did. This flightless bird, once found on the island of Mauritius, vanished in the 1600s—making it a symbol of extinction and mystery. No one alive today has ever seen a dodo in person, so it feels more like a legend than a fact. Some old drawings even show it with wings way too big!

🔥 The Phoenix: Born From Ashes

With feathers of flame and a cry like a song of fire, the phoenix is one of the most famous mythical birds. It was said to live for hundreds of years before bursting into flames and

Ethereal Ray

rising again, reborn from its ashes. Cultures around the world—from Ancient Egypt to China—had their own versions of this fiery flier. It's a symbol of renewal, hope, and rising again no matter what.

Thunderbird Returns

You may remember the Thunderbird from earlier—it's too powerful to mention just once! In many Native American stories, this mighty bird rules the skies and brings thunder and lightning with the flap of its wings. It's both fearsome and sacred, watching over the people below.

Garuda: Winged Guardian of the Gods

In Hindu and Buddhist traditions, Garuda is a giant eagle-like creature who serves as a guardian and divine messenger. With a golden body and incredible speed, he's said to carry gods through the heavens and battle evil forces in the skies.

Roc: The Elephant-Lifting Giant

Tales from the Middle East and South Asia describe a bird so huge it could lift elephants—yes, elephants! This was the Roc, featured in stories like *One Thousand and One Nights*. Some think ancient sailors might've seen real birds like condors or giant extinct species... and let their imaginations fly even higher.

Nimbus Fact!
The phoenix might be fiction—but some scientists think the idea of a bird rising from fire was inspired by real birds nesting near volcanoes or in hot, smoky places. Nature always has a spark of myth!

Ethereal Ray

❓ What's Real? What's Magic?

The line between science and myth isn't always clear—and that's okay! Many sky mysteries led to amazing discoveries. Legends inspired early scientists to ask questions, explore space, and even fly!

"Even today," Zephyr says, *"there's still magic in the sky. Whether you believe in dragons or data, the sky invites you to wonder. So... what do **you** believe might be out there?"*

🔭 Fun Sky Facts

- The word *"eclipse"* comes from a Greek word meaning "to leave or abandon."
- Some early sky maps included dragons and sea monsters in the constellations!
- In Norse mythology, the rainbow was a magical bridge called **Bifröst** that connected Earth to the realm of the gods.
- Comets used to be called "hairy stars" and were thought to predict big events.

- The longest-lasting visible UFO sighting happened in 1981 in France—and is still unsolved!

🌬 Closing Wonder

From ancient stories to modern mysteries, the sky has always been a place where imagination takes flight. We may understand more of it today—but there will always be room for wonder.

"Legends may live in the past, but curiosity lives forever," Zephyr smiles. *"And the sky? It's still full of secrets waiting for you to uncover."*

Chapter 10:
The Future of the Sky

"Strap in—this ride is heading to tomorrow!"

Nimbus and I are gazing at solar-powered planes and flying taxis—and beyond them, rockets launching into space. The sky of the future is full of possibilities. What inventions are on the horizon?

Could you be one of the next sky explorers? Let's look ahead to what's coming next.

Flying Cars & Sky Taxis

- The future might look a lot like your favorite sci-fi movie! Companies around the world are already testing **flying cars** and **air taxis**.
- These vehicles don't need roads—just airspace. Many are electric and eco-friendly.
- Some use **vertical takeoff and landing (VTOL)** tech—no runway needed!

Imagine calling an air taxi on your phone and zipping over traffic. Wild, right?

Floating Cities & Sky Homes

- Scientists and designers are dreaming up **floating homes**, sky platforms, and high-altitude living spaces.
- Ideas include **sky farms, wind-powered towers**, and even **balloon-supported cities** that hover above Earth.
- These could help with overcrowded cities or rising sea levels.

Drones That Do It All

- Drones aren't just for photos anymore! In the future, they could:
    - Deliver packages, food, or medicine
    - Fight wildfires from above
    - Monitor weather or pollution in real-time
    - Even help in rescue missions!

Some even imagine **drone highways in the sky**, with invisible lanes and traffic lights.

Sky Bridges to Space

- Engineers are working on **space elevators**—giant towers that could carry people or cargo from Earth into space!
- Instead of launching rockets, you'd ride an elevator into orbit. It sounds like sci-fi, but the science is in the works.
- Future skyports may connect air travel to space travel!

Greener, Cleaner Skies

- The sky of the future isn't just exciting—it's **sustainable:**
    - **Electric planes** and **solar-powered aircraft** are already being tested.
    - Eco-friendly fuels and quieter engines will make flying better for the planet.
    - Cloud tech might even help us control weather—or prevent disasters!

AI in the Sky

- Artificial intelligence is changing flight:
    - Planes that can fly themselves
    - Smart systems that predict storms
    - AI that helps air traffic control manage hundreds of flying vehicles at once!

Nimbus says: *"I'm not worried—I'm still the better co-pilot."*

What Will YOU Create?

"The sky of the future isn't just something you watch—it's something you'll shape," Zephyr says.
Maybe **you** will be the one to:

- Build a new kind of plane
- Invent weather-proof sky suits
- Help people live among the clouds
- Discover a mystery no one's solved yet!

Final Sky Facts

• The world's first all-electric passenger plane had its test flight in 2020!
• Japan plans to build a space elevator by the 2050s.
• The Airbus "Flying Whale" is a future plane designed to carry huge cargo gently through the skies.
• NASA is developing **quiet supersonic jets**—fast, but no big booms!
• Solar planes can fly for weeks without landing.

Zephyr's Farewell

"And just like that... our sky journey ends—but your adventure is just beginning," says Zephyr, gliding into the clouds with Nimbus.

"You've explored the layers, chased birds, danced with clouds, and imagined the future. Now, the sky belongs to you. Keep your eyes up, your heart open, and your dreams as high as the stars."

The sky isn't the limit. It's just the beginning.

Sky Explorer Lab

1. Make Your Own Cloud in a Jar

Materials:

- A glass jar with a lid
- Hot water
- Ice cubes
- Hairspray

Instructions:

1. Pour hot water into the jar until it's about 1/3 full.
2. Swirl the water around to warm the sides.
3. Turn the lid upside down and place a few ice cubes on top.
4. Quickly spray a bit of hairspray into the jar and place the lid (with ice) back on.
5. Watch your cloud form inside the jar!

2. Paper Airplane Distance Challenge

Materials:

- Paper (A4 or letter size)
- Markers or crayons
- Measuring tape
- Notebook and pen

Instructions:

1. Fold different styles of paper airplanes.
2. Decorate them with your own sky-themed designs!
3. Fly them in an open space and measure how far each one goes.
4. Record your results and experiment with different designs to see which flies the farthest.

3. Weather Journal

Materials:

- Notebook or printed template
- Pencils, crayons, markers
- Access to weather updates (TV, app, or newspaper)

Instructions:

1. Create a daily log for temperature, cloud type, wind speed, and precipitation.
2. Draw what the sky looks like each day.
3. Write a short weather prediction based on patterns you notice.

4. Sky Scavenger Hunt

Materials:

- Printable checklist or notebook
- Pen/pencil

Instructions:

1. Go outside and search the sky for:
    - A bird
    - A fluffy cloud
    - A plane

        - A jet trail
        - A balloon
        - The sun or moon
2. Check off each one and draw or describe what you saw.

5. Build a Mini Parachute

Materials:

- Plastic bag
- String
- Paper cup or small toy
- Scissors
- Tape

Instructions:

1. Cut a square from the plastic bag (about 12"x12").
2. Tape four pieces of string to the corners.
3. Tie the other ends of the strings to a small toy or paper cup.
4. Drop your parachute from a height and watch it float!

6. Tornado in a Bottle

Materials:

- 2 plastic bottles
- Water
- Glitter (optional)
- Duct tape
- Washer or tornado connector

Instructions:

1. Fill one bottle 3/4 full with water.
2. Add glitter if you like.
3. Attach the other bottle upside down using the washer or tape them together tightly.
4. Flip and swirl to create a spinning tornado!

7. Constellation Viewer

Materials:

- Empty toilet paper roll
- Black paper
- Push pin
- Tape
- Flashlight

Instructions:

1. Cut a small circle of black paper and poke holes in it to form a constellation pattern.
2. Tape it over one end of the roll.
3. In a dark room, shine a flashlight through the open end onto a wall.
4. Watch the constellation appear!

8. Create a Rain Gauge

Materials:

- A clear plastic bottle
- Ruler
- Marker
- Scissors
- Pebbles or stones

Instructions:

1. Cut the top off the bottle.
2. Fill the bottom with a few stones to keep it from tipping.
3. Turn the top upside down like a funnel and place it inside the bottle.
4. Use the marker to mark height lines with a ruler.
5. Leave it outside and check after it rains to measure precipitation!

9. Build & Fly a Simple Kite

Materials:

- Wooden skewers or thin dowels
- String
- Plastic bag or tissue paper
- Tape and scissors

Instructions:

1. Build a cross frame with the sticks and tape them together.
2. Cut the sail (kite body) from your bag or paper and tape it to the frame.
3. Tie string to the center where the sticks cross.
4. Fly it on a breezy day!

10. Sun Tracker Experiment

Materials:

- Paper plate
- Pencil or straw
- Clock
- Marker

Instructions:

1. Stick the pencil straight through the center of the paper plate.
2. Place it outside in the sun, flat side down.
3. Every hour, mark where the shadow falls and write the time.
4. Observe how the sun moves across the sky!

11. Make a Weather Barometer

Materials:

- Glass jar
- Balloon
- Rubber band
- Straw
- Paper and tape

Instructions:

1. Cut the balloon and stretch it over the jar opening.
2. Tape one end of the straw to the center of the balloon.
3. Tape a paper behind the straw as a scale.
4. Watch the straw move as air pressure changes!

12. Bird Watching Logbook

Materials:

- Notebook or printout
- Binoculars (optional)
- Pen or pencil

Instructions:

1. Sit outside and quietly observe birds.
2. Record what you see: size, color, sound, and behavior.
3. Try identifying birds using a guidebook or app!

13. Moon Phase Tracker

Materials:

- Calendar or printed tracker
- Pencil or crayons

Instructions:

1. Look at the moon each night for a month.
2. Draw the moon's shape for each night in your tracker.
3. Notice the full moon, new moon, and everything in between!

14. DIY Stargazing Night

Materials:

- Blanket
- Flashlight (red light if possible)
- Star chart app or printed map

Instructions:

1. Head outside on a clear night away from city lights.
2. Lay back, let your eyes adjust, and identify stars and constellations.
3. Use a star chart to guide your search. Try spotting a planet or satellite too!

Ethereal Ray

15. Wind Sock Craft

Materials:

- Paper or fabric
- String
- Tape or glue
- Stick or dowel

Instructions:

1. Decorate the paper with sky colors or weather symbols.
2. Roll it into a tube and secure it with tape.
3. Cut streamers for the bottom and attach with tape.
4. Tie string to the top and hang it on a stick. Watch it blow in the wind!

The Ultimate Sky Quiz

1. What is the sky mostly made of?
a) Fire
b) Water
c) Gases like oxygen and nitrogen
d) Sound waves
Reference Chapter: 1 (The Sky Above Us!)

2. Which layer of the atmosphere do we live in?
a) Exosphere
b) Mesosphere
c) Thermosphere
d) Troposphere
Reference Chapter: 1

3. What causes the sky to appear blue?
a) The ocean reflects its color
b) Clouds scatter light
c) Sunlight scatters through air molecules
d) The Moon shines blue light
Reference Chapter: 1

4. Which bird is the fastest in a dive?
a) Eagle

b) Peregrine falcon
c) Hummingbird
d) Hawk
Reference Chapter: 2 (Birds of the Sky)

5. Which bird flies the highest?
a) Albatross
b) Owl
c) Rüppell's vulture
d) Penguin
Reference Chapter: 2

6. Which bird has the longest migration journey?
a) Sparrow
b) Arctic tern
c) Crow
d) Peacock
Reference Chapter: 2

7. What type of bird can mimic human speech?
a) Parrot
b) Owl
c) Robin
d) Swan
Reference Chapter: 2

8. What are clouds made of?
a) Dust
b) Air bubbles
c) Water droplets or ice crystals
d) Cotton
Reference Chapter: 3 (Soaring Through the Clouds)

9. Which cloud type is flat and gray, often bringing drizzle?
a) Cumulus
b) Stratus
c) Cirrus
d) Lenticular
Reference Chapter: 3

10. What does a cumulonimbus cloud usually bring?
a) Sunny skies
b) Gentle breeze
c) Thunderstorms
d) Snowflakes
Reference Chapter: 3

11. Who were the first to fly a powered airplane?
a) Montgolfier brothers
b) Wright brothers
c) Leonardo da Vinci
d) Charles Lindbergh
Reference Chapter: 4 (Amazing Airplanes)

12. What force pushes an airplane upward?
a) Gravity
b) Thrust
c) Drag
d) Lift
Reference Chapter: 4

13. What is the name of the plane powered by solar energy that flew around the world?
a) Voyager
b) Concorde
c) Solar Impulse 2
d) Sky Flyer
Reference Chapter: 4

14. What makes a hot air balloon rise?
a) Helium
b) Jet engine
c) Cold air
d) Warm air is lighter than cool air
Reference Chapter: 5 (Hot Air Balloons & Blimps)

15. What type of airship had the tragic Hindenburg disaster?
a) Jet
b) Helicopter
c) Zeppelin

d) Drone
Reference Chapter: 5

16. What flying machine uses flapping wings like a bird?
a) Glider
b) Ornithopter
c) Rocket
d) Kite
Reference Chapter: 5

17. What is the day-to-day condition of the atmosphere called?
a) Season
b) Sky phase
c) Weather
d) Climate
Reference Chapter: 6 (Extreme Weather Wonders)

18. What causes thunder?
a) Wind
b) Clouds colliding
c) Lightning heating the air
d) Rain hitting the ground
Reference Chapter: 6

19. What's the calm part at the center of a hurricane called?
a) Spiral
b) Eye
c) Funnel
d) Head
Reference Chapter: 6

20. What is fog?
a) Rain
b) Dust cloud
c) A low cloud
d) Dry wind
Reference Chapter: 6

21. Which is the only flying mammal?
a) Squirrel
b) Bat
c) Eagle
d) Lemur
Reference Chapter: 7 (Creatures That Fly But Aren't Birds)

22. What do dragonflies and bees have in common?
a) Big eyes
b) Strong beaks
c) Four wings
d) Night vision
Reference Chapter: 7

23. What sea creature can "fly" above water to escape predators?
a) Squid
b) Jellyfish
c) Flying fish
d) Octopus
Reference Chapter: 7

24. What do ornithologists study?
a) Stars
b) Weather
c) Airplanes
d) Birds
Reference Chapter: 8 (Sky Careers)

25. Who helps airplanes take off and land safely?
a) Flight attendant
b) Air traffic controller
c) Pilot assistant
d) Sky ranger
Reference Chapter: 8

26. What do meteorologists study?
a) Meteors
b) Ocean waves
c) Weather patterns

d) Satellites
Reference Chapter: 8

27. What mythical bird is said to rise from its own ashes?
a) Roc
b) Thunderbird
c) Dodo
d) Phoenix
Reference Chapter: 9 (Myths & Legends)

28. What glowing lights appear in the polar skies?
a) Fireflies
b) Aurora Borealis
c) Sundogs
d) Fire clouds
Reference Chapter: 9

29. What are constellations?
a) Star maps
b) Flying objects
c) Moon craters
d) Clouds
Reference Chapter: 9

30. What future invention might connect Earth to space like an elevator?
a) Sky ladder

b) Space bridge
c) Rocket tunnel
d) Space elevator
Reference Chapter: 10 (The Future of the Sky)

✅ Answer Key - Sky Quiz

1. **c)** Gases like oxygen and nitrogen
2. **d)** Troposphere
3. **c)** Sunlight scatters through air molecules
4. **b)** Peregrine falcon
5. **c)** Rüppell's vulture
6. **b)** Arctic tern
7. **a)** Parrot
8. **c)** Water droplets or ice crystals
9. **b)** Stratus
10. **c)** Thunderstorms
11. **b)** Wright brothers
12. **d)** Lift
13. **c)** Solar Impulse 2
14. **d)** Warm air is lighter than cool air
15. **c)** Zeppelin
16. **b)** Ornithopter
17. **c)** Weather
18. **c)** Lightning heating the air
19. **b)** Eye
20. **c)** A low cloud
21. **b)** Bat
22. **c)** Four wings
23. **c)** Flying fish
24. **d)** Birds
25. **b)** Air traffic controller
26. **c)** Weather patterns

Ethereal Ray

27. **d**) Phoenix
28. **b**) Aurora Borealis
29. **a**) Star maps
30. **d**) Space elevator

The Ultimate Sky Facts for Kids, Teens, & Adults

Glossary of Sky Terms

▫ **Atmosphere** – The layers of gases surrounding Earth.

▫ **Troposphere** – The lowest layer of the atmosphere, where weather happens.

▫ **Stratosphere** – The layer above the troposphere, containing the ozone layer.

▫ **Mesosphere** – The middle layer where meteors often burn up.

▫ **Thermosphere** – The layer where the auroras and the ISS are found.

▫ **Exosphere** – The outermost layer of the atmosphere, where satellites orbit.

▫ **Aurora Borealis** – Colorful lights caused by particles from the Sun hitting Earth's atmosphere (also called the Northern Lights).

▫ **Cloud** – A mass of water droplets or ice crystals floating in the sky.

▫ **Cumulonimbus** – A tall, storm-producing cloud that can bring thunder and lightning.

▫ **Cirrus** – Thin, wispy clouds high in the sky.

Ethereal Ray

- **Weather** – Day-to-day atmospheric conditions.

- **Climate** – Long-term weather patterns in a region.

- **Rain** – Water droplets that fall from clouds.

- **Snow** – Ice crystals that fall when it's cold.

- **Hail** – Balls of ice that fall during storms.

- **Lightning** – A powerful flash of electricity in the sky.

- **Thunder** – The sound made when lightning superheats the air.

- **Tornado** – A rotating column of air touching the ground from a storm.

- **Hurricane** – A massive storm system with strong winds and rain.

- **Fog** – A low-lying cloud near the ground.

- **Lift** – The force that helps an airplane rise.

- **Thrust** – The forward force produced by an engine.

- **Drag** – Air resistance pushing against a flying object.

- **Glider** – A light aircraft with no engine that soars on air currents.

- **Parachute** – A device that slows a fall by creating air resistance.

- **Drone** – A remote-controlled flying machine.

- **Ornithologist** – A scientist who studies birds.

- **Meteorologist** – A scientist who studies weather.

- **Constellation** – A group of stars forming a recognizable pattern.

- **UFO** – Unidentified Flying Object.

- **Phoenix** – A mythical firebird that is reborn from its ashes.

- **Zephyr** – A gentle breeze (also the name of your sky guide!)

- **Nimbus** – A type of rain cloud (and Zephyr's flying friend!)

What's YOUR Sky Discovery?

You've traveled through clouds, chased storms, met feathered flyers, and explored the future of flight. Now it's your turn to become the sky explorer!

Write or draw something cool you discovered while reading this book.
It could be:

- Your favorite sky fact
- A bird or cloud that amazed you
- A flying invention idea
- A made-up sky creature you imagined!

Zephyr says: "The sky's not the limit—it's just the beginning. Your curiosity can take you even higher!"

Draw here or use this space to write your sky thoughts and dreams:

The Ultimate Sky Facts for Kids, Teens, & Adults

Review Request

☁️ **Did this book make your imagination take flight?**

If so, Nimbus and I would love to hear from you! Your review on Amazon or Goodreads helps other sky explorers discover the wonders above—and inspires us to keep chasing clouds, stars, and stories through the sky!

📸 **Share your favorite discoveries!**
If you had fun soaring through these sky facts, consider uploading a photo or video with your Amazon review! Maybe it's your favorite sky creature, an awesome airplane drawing, or even a cloud shape that sparked your imagination—we'd love to see it! 🕊️

Leave a review by scanning the QR code below!

Your words help us keep exploring and may even spark the next volume of *The Ultimate Sky Facts Book*!

Thank you for flying with us—stay curious, keep looking up, and never stop wondering about the sky's endless possibilities! 🌈

The Ultimate Sky Facts for Kids, Teens, & Adults

Check my growing book series!

ELEVEN BOOKS TO EXPLORE

Scan the QR below

Printed in Great Britain
by Amazon